I LOVE THE NEW BABY AT OUR HOUSE...

Most of the Time

Leslie Kimmelman

Illustrations by Cynthia Jabar

A PERIGEE BOOK

Write your name—or have a parent write
your name—in your favorite color. Then turn
the pages and use any space to write and
color about your fantastic family.

THIS BOOK BELONGS TO

A PERIGEE BOOK
Published by the Penguin Group
Penguin Group (USA) Inc.
375 Hudson Street, New York, New York 10014, USA
Penguin Group (Canada), 90 Eglinton Avenue East, Suite 700, Toronto, Ontario M4P 2Y3, Canada
(a division of Pearson Penguin Canada Inc.)
Penguin Books Ltd., 80 Strand, London WC2R 0RL, England
Penguin Group Ireland, 25 St. Stephen's Green, Dublin 2, Ireland (a division of Penguin Books Ltd.)
Penguin Group (Australia), 250 Camberwell Road, Camberwell, Victoria 3124, Australia
(a division of Pearson Australia Group Pty. Ltd.)
Penguin Books India Pvt. Ltd., 11 Community Centre, Panchsheel Park, New Delhi—110 017, India
Penguin Group (NZ), 67 Apollo Drive, Rosedale, North Shore 0632, New Zealand
(a division of Pearson New Zealand Ltd.)
Penguin Books (South Africa) (Pty.) Ltd., 24 Sturdee Avenue, Rosebank, Johannesburg 2196, South Africa

Penguin Books Ltd., Registered Offices: 80 Strand, London WC2R 0RL, England

I LOVE THE NEW BABY AT OUR HOUSE...MOST OF THE TIME

Text copyright © 2009 by Leslie Kimmelman
Illustrations copyright © 2009 by Cynthia Jabar
Cover art and design by Cynthia Jabar

First edition: June 2009

ISBN: 978-0-399-53500-0

PRINTED IN THE UNITED STATES OF AMERICA

10 9 8 7 6 5 4 3 2 1

Most Perigee books are available at special quantity discounts for bulk purchases for sales promotions,
premiums, fund-raising, or educational use. Special books, or book excerpts, can also be created to fit
specific needs. For details, write: Special Markets, Penguin Group (USA) Inc., 375 Hudson Street, New
York, New York 10014.

CHAPTER ONE
OUR BRAND-NEW BABY

THIS IS ME.

My name is _ _ _ _ _ _ _ _ _ _ _ _ _ _ _ _ _ _

I am a

☐ **BOY**

☑ **GIRL**

This is what I looked like when I was a baby. I was cute!

This is what the new baby in our family looks like.

The baby's name is ___ALEXANDRA___.

(_____ would have been a good name, too.

But not ___MICHAELA___.

That would've been a silly name!)

The baby is a

☐ BOY

 GIRL

THE BABY WAS BORN

- ☐ IN THE MORNING
- ☐ IN THE AFTERNOON
- ☑ AT NIGHT

on ___FEB 9_____, 20 _11___.

So that is Baby's birthday.

MY BIRTHDAY IS ____MARCH 27____.

I am ___2½_____ years old.

I will put _3___ candles on my next birthday cake because that's how old I will be.

_____ OMA _____ **took care of me when Baby was being born.**

Here is a picture of what we did while we waited.

(we were hugging)

THE FIRST TIME I SAW BABY WAS

- ☑ **AT THE HOSPITAL**
- ☐ **AT HOME**
- ☐ _____

Baby looked as

- ☐ **CUTE AS A PUPPY**
- ☐ **TINY AS A MEATBALL**
- ☐ **WRINKLED AS AN ELEPHANT**
- ☐ **RED AS A STRAWBERRY**
- ☑ CUTE AS A BABY _____

BABY CAME HOME.

The day was

- ☐ SUNNY
- ☐ CLOUDY
- ☐ RAINY
- ☒ SNOWY

Draw the weather.

HOME

THE FIRST THING BABY DID WAS

- [ ] SLEEP
- [ ] CRY
- [ ] PEE
- [x] BURP
- [x] SPIT UP

Draw a welcome sign.

WHERE DOES BABY SLEEP?

 THERE'S A ROOM JUST FOR BABY.

 BABY SHARES A ROOM WITH __MOMMY__.

This is what it looks like.

BABY'S FIRST BATH WAS IN

- ☐ A BIG BATHTUB
- ☒ A LITTLE BABY-SIZE BATHTUB
- ☒ THE SINK
- ☐ A GOLDFISH BOWL

I help with Baby's bath.

I help by _Washing her head_

and _her belly & legs & feet_.

I do NOT help to change Baby's diaper.
Too smelly!

Baby's eyes are

- ☒ BLUE
- ☐ BROWN
- ☐ GREEN

Baby's hair is

- ☐ BLOND
- ☐ RED
- ☐ BLACK
- ☒ BROWN
- ☐ NO HAIR AT ALL!

MY BABY

Baby was _____20.5_____ inches tall and
weighed _____9_____ pounds, _____5_____ ounces
at birth.

My eyes are
- [ ] BLUE
- [ ] BROWN
- [x] GREEN

My hair is
- [ ] BLOND
- [ ] RED
- [ ] BLACK
- [x] BROWN
- [ ] NO HAIR AT ALL!

ME

Now I am ___38___ inches tall
and weigh ___31___ pounds.

OUR FAMILY TREE

Without the new baby, I wouldn't be a big

☐ **BROTHER**

☐ **SISTER**

Do apples grow on family trees?

How about ice cream cones or pizza pies?

Draw something tasty on your family tree!

Grandmother
ANTJE / KATHY

Grandmother
BETSY / CATHY

Grandfather
DAVE

Grandfather
CRAIG

Mom
KATIE

Dad
ISAAC

Me :)
MICHAELA

Baby
ALEXANDA

We also have a pet

- [ ] DOG
- [x] CAT
- [ ] CANARY
- [ ] FISH
- [ ] HORSE
- [ ] GUINEA PIG
- [ ] HIPPOPOTAMUS
- [ ] _____

It is named _____PUNKY_____.

We do not have a pet,
but I wish we had
a _____ for a pet.

Draw your real or imaginary pet here.

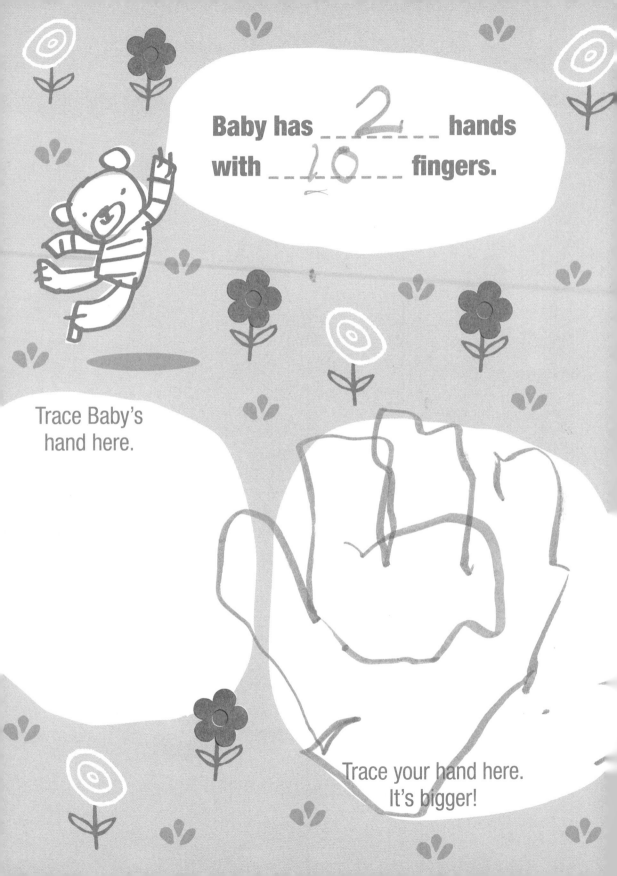

Baby has __2__ hands with __10__ fingers.

Trace Baby's hand here.

Trace your hand here. It's bigger!

Baby has __2__ feet with __10__ toes.

Trace Baby's foot here.

Trace your foot here.
It's bigger!

Baby also has

_ _ _ _ head

_ _ _ _ eyes

_ _ _ _ nose

_ _ _ _ ears and

_ _ _ _ belly button/s.

So do I.

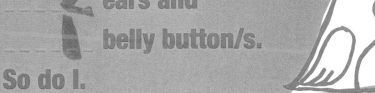

Write your own message here.

This is what I'd look like if I had two heads—or five belly buttons!

Does Baby have teeth?

Nope, not yet!

But I do! I have _____ teeth on top,

and __ 10 ____ teeth below.

I also have a tongue.

And I

☐ CAN

☒ CANNOT but almost!

touch my tongue

to my nose.

Watch me touch my nose to this spot!

This is me and Baby together.

I like to play with Baby,
but Baby also spends a lot of time

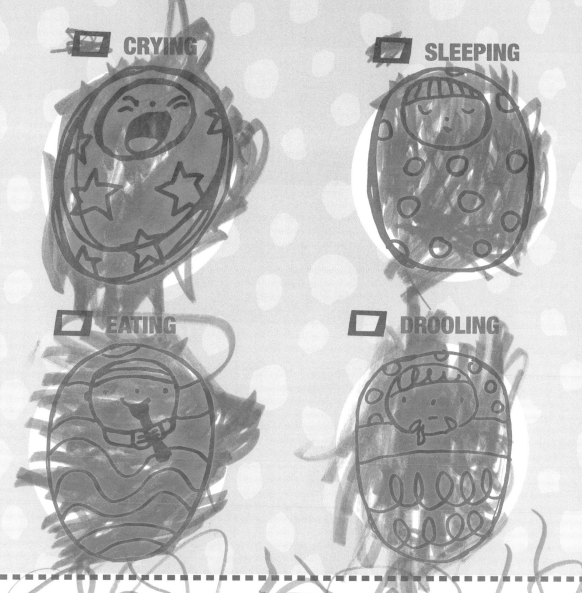

☐ CRYING

☐ SLEEPING

☐ EATING

☐ DROOLING

BORING! Not me.

My favorite things to do are _Play with my_

and _Dad!_____ .

But sometimes everyone is so busy with BABY that I feel invisible. That means it feels like no one notices I'm here, or even sees me at all.

This is a picture of me being invisible. Can't see me on this page? That's because I am invisible.

If I could really be invisible, I would

☐ **DISAPPEAR WHEN IT'S TIME TO CLEAN MY ROOM**

☐ **SNEAK OUT OF BED TO SEE WHAT MY PARENTS DO AFTER I GO TO SLEEP**

☐ **EAT A SECOND, THIRD, AND FOURTH HELPING OF FUDGE CAKE**

☐ And lots of cheese, yogurt + crackers

(Write your own answer here.)

Sometimes I wish that I were the baby again, so I could get all of the attention. But most of the time, I'm happy to be the older child.

Decorate these shirts!

Baby's first word was _____,
spoken on _____, 20 _____.
Now Baby is learning new words, too,
like _____
and _____.
I asked my parents, and they told me my
first word was _____.

I'm learning big words now, like
☑ **TYRANNOSAURUS REX**
☑ **RAVIOLI**
☑ **ESCALATOR**
☑ **AMBULANCE**
☑ **FABRIC SOFTENER**
☐ _____
(Write your own answer here.)

Baby's favorite foods are _ _ _ _ _ _ _ _ _ _ _ _ _ _ _ _
and _ .

But definitely not _ _ _ _ _ _ _ _ _ _ _ _ _ _ _ _ _ _ !

Baby sometimes wears food,
instead of eating it.

My favorite foods are
BANANA BABY FOOD, MEAT and
CRACKERS CHEESE YOGURT
But if I see _____ CELERY _____
on the plate, I say "no thanks!" and
shut my mouth tight!

Draw your favorite food.

Guess which one of us is
the messiest eater?

BABY CRIES

 SOMETIMES

 A LOT

The crying sounds like

 A TINY KITTEN

A ROARING LION

A FIRE ENGINE

**I DON'T KNOW BECAUSE
I HAVE MY FINGERS IN MY EARS**

BABY LIKES WHEN WE SING!

Baby's favorite songs are TWINKLE LITTLE STAR

and ROCK A BYE BABY.

My favorite songs are BINGO

and OLD MCDONALD.

BABY LIKES LOOKING AT BOOKS!

Baby's favorite books are

and

My favorite books are DISNEY BOOKS

and ALL OF THEM!

BABY FIRST crawls

on _ _ _ _ _ _ _ _ _ _ _ _, 20 _ _ _ _ _.

BABY TAKES FIRST steps

on _ _ _ _ _ _ _ _ _ _ _ _ _, 20 _ _ _ _ _.

I can move lots of other ways, too.

I can

 JUMP

 HOP

 SKIP

 WALK BACKWARD

 GALLOP

 SLITHER LIKE A SNAKE

BABY'S FIRST tooth came in
on _ _ _ _ _ _ _ _ _ _ _, 20 _ _ _ _.

BABY'S FIRST haircut was
on _ _ _ _ _ _ _ _ _ _, 20 _ _ _ _.

Tape a lock of Baby's hair here.

Baby's first drawing was
on _ _ _ _ _ _ _ _ _ _, 20 _ _ _ _.

(I ☐ DID ☐ DID NOT
help Baby scribble.)

On Baby's first birthday, _____

and _____ came.

We celebrated by _____

and _____.

We decorated with _____

and _____.

We ate _____ -flavored

cake with _____ icing.

Happy 1st Birthday!

CHAPTER THREE
BABY DREAMS

You are so lucky to be in this family, Baby.
And we are so lucky to have you!
Here is a picture of all of us together.

HERE ARE SOME IMPORTANT THINGS TO KNOW.

The greatest thing about this family is

CAUSE I LIKE THE BABY
(+ love)

Our favorite thing to do together is

STICKER BOOK

On really special days, we

PLAY SOCCER, GO IN POOL

When we want to be really SILLY, we

The best thing about MOM is
I LOVE YOU + LOVE ~~HUGGING~~

The best thing about DAD is
I HUG + KISS HIM ALL OVER

The best thing about ME is
I LIKE HUGGING + KISSING
MY BABY SISTER

The best thing about BABY is
NOTHING, I JUST LIKE HER

PROUD FACE

Mostly I feel happy, but not always.
You need to know all these faces, so you can
recognize me no matter what.

HAPPY FACE

SAD FACE

k tears

SCARED FACE

MAD FACE

PROUD FACE

FUNNY FACE

There are so many things I'm going to teach you when you get a little older.

I'LL TEACH YOU TO

- ☐ TIE YOUR SHOES
- ☐ RIDE A BIKE
- ☐ COUNT TO TEN
- ☐ WRITE YOUR NAME
- ☐ BUILD A SNOWMAN
- ☐ CATCH A BALL
- ☐ TWIRL SPAGHETTI ON A FORK
- ☐ DANCE THE FUNKY CHICKEN
- ☐ SNEAK ICKY LIMA BEANS INTO THE TRASH

1, 2, 3, 4, 5...

I'll also teach you to

MAKE FUNNY FACES

and CURL HER TONGUE

BUT FOR NOW, I CAN

- ☑ MAKE FUNNY FACES TO MAKE YOU LAUGH
- ☑ HOLD YOUR HAND
- ☑ COVER YOU WITH YOUR BLANKIE
- ☑ SING YOUR FAVORITE SONG
- ☑ BRING YOU YOUR BINKIE
- ☑ TRY NOT TO MIND WHEN YOU CRY

I can also

_____ PLAY WITH HER _____

and _____.

WELCOME TO OUR FAMILY, BABY!

We love you

☐ UP TO THE STARS AND TO THE MOON

☐ DOWN TO THE BOTTOM OF THE OCEAN

☐ AROUND THE WHOLE EARTH A GAJILLION TIMES

☐ AS MUCH AS 37 ICE CREAM SUNDAES WITH WHIPPED CREAM AND RAINBOW SPRINKLES AND A CHERRY ON TOP